The Book of Good Dreams

New and Selected Poems

by

Douglas Richardson

Also by Douglas Richardson

Fiction:
Trust Fund Baby
The Corruption of Zachary R.

Poetry:
Ghosts in Time and Space
Poems for Loners
Out in the Cold, Cold Day
Sugar Fish

The Book of Good Dreams

New and Selected Poems

by

Douglas Richardson

Weak Creature Press
Los Angeles

The Book of Good Dreams
©2014 by Douglas Richardson
Weak Creature Press

This is a work of poetry. Any resemblance to actual persons, living or deceased, events, or locations is entirely coincidental.

Library of Congress Control Number: 2014900346
ISBN: 978-0-9842424-6-7

Printed in the United States of America.

Cover design by Heather DeSerio, Precision Edge Design LLC.

Cover photo by Douglas Richardson.

Author photo by Prudence Smuggery.

For information on other publications available from Weak Creature Press, please email weakcreature@aol.com.

Contents

Awards and Acknowledgments

About the Author

Also by Weak Creature Press

For Jen

The Book of Good
Dreams (*new poems*)

Siberian Summer

you check in
at the wooden gate
the lake beyond
has thawed
the sunlight upon it
seems to speak
it says
the burden is gone

Transient Triptych

1.
there are fountains in the statue garden
but a guard dog keeps you out
you worry about trees in the winter
you worry about yourself in the winter

2.
a Shell station on the corner
in the new century
same architecture as the last century
but not the next

3.
there are twenty-six beds
in the mattress showroom
you can sleep there tonight
until they see you in the light

Sidetracked

feeling desperate
about the number
of missing children
I drove off
in my car
to find a new city
but was sidetracked
by the rows
between trees
in an orchard
and wandered off
on foot
instead

A Laundromat

a laundromat
in the starry night
just you and a woman
who looks familiar
she hums a melody
that travels
like myth
down your spine
your clothes spinning
safe and warm
in the machines

A Wayward Son

Though your earnestness was never questioned,
you spent all your years becoming an expert in
arcana for which no employer would pay a wage.
Now, thanks to you, the town is in perpetual
darkness. You think the children should be afraid
of you, but a boy gives you his bicycle. You flip it
upside down and crank the pedal. The free-
spinning wheel lights up the sky and churns
barrels of the finest ice cream.

At the Starting Line

From our vantage point at the starting line, we can see how the coastline shapes the bay. The race official points across the water to a mountain on the faraway shore and announces that we will run until we collapse into the arms of the Virgen de Guadalupe.

If Your Ways Are Right

If your ways are right, mere acquaintances in
your waking life may be kinder in your dreams.
They may wait in the kitchen for your bread to
toast, then offer you a stick of gum in an office
lobby, then sit with you at a funeral where
nobody likes you. But if your ways are wrong,
they may reach inside your cab in heavy traffic in
a city that smells like piss and bludgeon you with
psychopathic fists, all because of what you have
done, which you did knowingly without
mitigating prayer.

Because You Like Music

for a limited time only
in the timelessness of sleep
because you like music
and champion the weak
you will be transported
to where things
have been known all along
to hear your favorite song
which was written
after you were gone

You Survived the Ordeal

now red wine
stains a cork
the heat of it
in the afternoon
your mind
quiet enough
for fire

Medicine Cabinet

in the bathroom
you open the medicine cabinet
and watch your face multiply
as one mirror closes in on the other
losing your friends
and the park outside

The Jogger

You could have met her at a wedding reception or
seen her in a party of strangers looking out a
window with a drink in her hand and you were
just passing by on the street below and decided to
go up, but she said excuse me or pardon and
jogged by to the music in her headphones under
the moon and Venus, which has no moon.

A Lucid Afternoon

On a lucid afternoon you sit at the kitchen table
writing a letter that details every essential
memory of your life—eating lemons, watching
game shows, and so on and so forth for forty-five
pages. You put it in an envelope and walk to the
post office. You feel different now, lighter. Your
back has stopped aching. You pass by the used
car lot. The cars have olive branches for antennas.
Your dinner and meds await back home, a photo
of your wife on the fridge.

A Lightning Storm

a lightning storm at night
and later a nurse asks
and you respond
in your mind
that your thoughts are the same
but your motor skills are shot
then you hear
in your own slurred speech
that the storm
was pretty to look at

American Train

how many miles
on
hundred-year lines
the generations
of
living pines in
silver granite
and
golden grass in
ancient desert
rail shining
on a summer night

how many miles
through
foreign cities
in the homeland
buildings lit up
in a starless sky
janitors adrift inside
dreaming
suburban foothills
coyotes
and
mice
at peace
on the quiet streets

how many miles
in the distance
of a child's
imagination
fading in and out
of vision
from the backseat
of a family vacation
different routes
to the same
destination

A Raft

a raft
in the open ocean
water the color of iron
rising and falling
death everywhere
below and unseen
the sky white
you look at the sky

Scent of the Ocean

scent of the ocean
in the middle of the room
and
all the accompanying colors
turns out your religion was true
all along

from Ghosts in Time
and Space (2011)

The First True Breath

My finest day as a groundwarmer
was the day I ceased to be one
a passing through
upon the miracle of death
which we all agree
was the first true breath

Ghosts, show them your stories
your poetic failures
your prosaic glories
frighten them if you must

Prove to them their waning faith
may be rekindled by a wraith

‡

Rattle

In the world I come from
we fall in love only once.

This does not mean mistakes
are not made
or are infrequent.

Our population is small
like your Wyoming,
and like Wyoming
the living and the deceased
haunt the land with equal skill.

Our world is cool and green
and our architects
are quite accomplished.

I don't travel much to other worlds;
I prefer to work like the bees
in our vast gardens,
as vast as your oceans.

Occasionally I rattle
a child's cup of cider;
this small thrill for the child
reminds me of my mistake.

Becoming

I awake on a stranger's lawn
in the Coachella Valley.
It's March 14, 2011.
Eighty-eight degrees will be the high.
The residents pass over
and through me and don't notice.
I should tell you this is not unusual.

I stand and walk to a bus stop,
no hunger and no thirst.
I see migrating geese cutting
in sharp formations,
becoming a school of fish in the sky.
I should tell you this is not possible.

The bus rides through five cities
along the base of the mountains,
past repeating resorts and cafés
and restaurants.
I stop in the same café in three different cities
because I like a room full of voices
other than my own.
I should tell you that I want to live again.

In the evening a brother and sister
play cards on a table outside,
no sound and nothing to burn.
I watch them from an empty parking lot

where the heat of the day still rises.
I should tell you that I rise along with it.

Scorn

for protection I kept a rusty nail
in a beat-up Betty Boop tote bag
and twirled my frizzy hair;
barnacles under the boardwalk
made me cry

my goal early in life was to spot
the farthest point I could see
and run away from it

my goal late in life was to return
to where I came from
using beer and antihistamines

drug-softened memories were so quiet
they kept me company
like faraway islands
and the
silent ocean between

Bakersfield

One morning I opened the newspaper
and saw the doe eyes of a drifter
who had passed away
on the side of a highway
near Bakersfield.

The photo had been taken
two years earlier
and was the last known
image of the man.

I never spoke again
for the rest of my days,
which really wasn't much of a feat
since I only lived another week.

When I was alive, I would have
passed him by with mean eyes.

This hurts my core even now.

I am desperate to find this man.

A newspaper blowing along the highway
in Bakersfield
means I am looking.

A New Town

In the city I searched
for a solitary painting,
a rain-blackened tree.
I held hot water in a paper cup,
avoided the hostile eyes of strangers.
Later I left town.
Long grass grew in the gravel
and made the sky turn gray.
Tar on telephone poles –
warm to the touch.
And then open desert.
Transmission towers stretched
into the distance,
past where I could see.
And then night –
almost black, with no mind.
Sleep was the strange night event.
Later I arrived in a new town.

The Seraph

I am the seraph in the faraway blue
I am 45 degrees Fahrenheit
give or take one or two
I am silent, not songless
I am disarming and miraculous
How can stars speak intimately
yet somehow they do
I am the seraph in the faraway blue

A Serious Boy

My aunts brought me
to Disneyland
when I was five.
I held tight
to the string
on my balloon,
but it slipped away when
I forgot about it.
I looked up in time
to see it disappear
into the sky.
I became a serious boy
after that day.
My aunts didn't seem
to understand
that I had died.

3:36

I lived my entire life in a hippie commune.
I don't have much to say about it,
but this doesn't mean I was dull
or without conviction.

I was born three months premature.
My mom ate poison mushrooms
and drank Southern Comfort
because she thought it would
make her more like Janis Joplin.

She was right.
Her singing voice improved
when she was hallucinating and drunk.

The commune midwife who delivered me
believed it wise to play music
for the mother-to-be in labor.
She played Janis Joplin, Neil Young,
the Byrds, and Led Zeppelin.

I came out of my mother's womb
to Zeppelin's "Going to California,"
a pretty song for acoustic guitar
three minutes and thirty-six seconds long.

When the song came to an end, so did I.
My mother followed the next day.
I lived my entire life in a hippie commune.

31

Spectrum

Poison mushrooms grew
on Damp Mountain
like quarter notes
and half notes
and whole,
so we ate them
and they made us
sing colors
all the way down
to the Bay:
red and orange,
gold and violet,
even S.F.P.D. blue,
which used its envy against us,
turned us green in the City
and made us impossible to hide.

My comrades and me and the boy in my belly
slept in jail that night, but justice in the morning
brought us back to Damp Mountain, which
trembled and flooded when my water broke.

My girlfriend played music from high above and I
sank into the canyon of birth. Black hours passed,
and then came white silence, and now I am mist
on Damp Mountain.

Hollywood Bowl

I reside at the Hollywood Bowl
on a summer evening
a helicopter high above and ascending
crickets on the perimeter and
the orchestra forever tuning

the audience is filing in
on the wind
on the wine
on their blankets

the symphony will not begin
until the last one is in
the orchestra forever tuning
a helicopter high above and ascending

Movements

groundwarmers in cars and
buses and trains
go from home to work and back again
ghosts through portals in time and walls
move through paintings in museum halls

stare at a painting with intensity
to spot ghosts on the go
catch Proust and his bossy great-aunt
in the clouds of "Woman with Parasol"
see Monet appear in a Pissarro
studying the colors in the streets below

the painters where
rue Saint Vincent meets
rue des Saules
were masters of great renown
their ghosts mimic groundwarmers
trudging their way through town
satisfied by the bump and strain

A Lifetime of Temporary Philosophies

Mine was a lifetime of temporary philosophies,
such as "allow your enemies to laugh in a crowd"
or "a case of Budweiser is a portly witch" or
"there is so much evil now, we can't even trust
the tap water" or "you can't commit suicide if
you don't exist."

Voltaire had an aphorism of his own: "A witty
saying proves nothing." This, ironically, was my
favorite. Somehow I knew I was no more than a
pigeon with a human head, or vice versa.

And somehow my shaky religions and my beer
left me hazy and bitter. I began voting
Republican. I got sober and went back to school.
I secured a steady job. Bought a small house.
Raked leaves. Talked to my plaid-shirted
neighbor.

But eventually this also left me hazy and bitter,
and vaguely suicidal, so I abandoned all and just
kept on living right through death, finally
understanding that life was not mine to take.

Paragenesis

My sister had a brood
I was barren
she was my tenant
I had her evicted

along with everyone else in the building
whom I deemed could breed

Then I lived alone
twenty-one doors
with twenty-one locks and keys

I gardened on my knees
among the toys and around the swings
that I made her abandon

At night I swung in the moonlight
watching the toys leap and roll
among my roses

Whose invisible brood could this be?
I wondered
and I tamped
their cuts and gashes
when they snagged the thorns

Then one morning
I woke with a strange head
that heard strange horns

and I stayed in bed
until the sun went down

At night I swing in the moonlight
with my visible brood

twenty-one children
with twenty-one locks and keys

The Staircase

Bicycles, carriages, cable cars. Anything to be in motion. Anything to escape my mortal heft.

A staircase in a turn-of-the-century apartment in San Francisco, narrow and musty, with doors at the top and bottom.

No one loitered there. Ladies didn't linger all defensive and mysterious. There was no railing for men to lean on and leer.

This was a tunnel for travel that echoed after each footfall, as if someone was right on your heels, or closer, as if someone was trying to invade you.

I lived in the room behind the top door until 1906, when the building and I went down in the quake. A new building went up in 1912, an exact replica of the old one. It is still there today.

I am there too: right on your heels, or closer, in the staircase.

The Scarecrow

I live in a field where darkness grows
we don't speak of immortality

Where has the light gone?
to the heavens, I suppose
and isn't that just vanity

But I've still got heroin, my
romantic heroine
and I've still got suicide, my
glamorous suicide
and I can still bring myself
to shake
in the shadows
with the crows

I live in a field where darkness grows
we don't speak of immortality

Dual

My eternal residence is
Los Angeles International Airport
I watch the planes take off
I watch the planes land
and besides that I amuse myself
by sliding down the luggage chutes
and flying the lengths of long corridors

There is no weather to distract me
from my placid mood
though I do like to look out
the windows on stormy days

I also like to hold
the passengers' coffee cups
and imagine the warmth
which I can no longer feel

I drank coffee until my 53rd birthday
which was the day I arrived

My sister died in a plane crash
when I was a boy
I never got to know her properly
because we were so young

My eternal residence is
Los Angeles International Airport
I watch the planes take off

I watch the planes land
and I wait for my sister

Duello

The adults called us the two translucent kids from the neighborhood. They said we had that otherworldly quality which would bring either great fortune or senseless tragedy.

My little brother and I were embarrassed by these grandiose observations. We knew we weren't the kids who would go out into the world and accomplish things or die trying. We weren't the kids who "knew" things. We wondered where knowledge came from, how people understood what to do in the physical world, which baffled the two of us.

That's why I confess I felt relieved when the DC-10 began its terminal descent into the Pacific Ocean twenty miles off the coast of Los Angeles. The anxiety over what I would fail to become vanished. Perhaps I was meant to become a child air crash victim.

I suspect my brother had similar feelings, though the postcrash effects on us have been curiously different. I am able to discern where my brother is and what he is thinking and doing at all times, and I have total recall of our lives and how they ended. My brother, however, thinks he lived to be fifty-three years old. The life he imagines he lived

is so extraordinary that I am still undecided
whether I should ever see him again.

My eternal residence is the flight paths and jet
streams over California. His eternal residence is
Los Angeles International Airport.

Kept Low

When I died, I asked to see Jesus
so I was sent to the Holy Land
during his time on earth.

I was ashamed and kept low in the Jordan
which pleased him,
and he filled me with his spirit
which made me cry.

His followers on the riverbank heard me
but because I was low
they thought I was a ripple in the water.

Corona

I always forgot about
the return of April
when I had to hear
that certain Doors song
about the mist burning off
and the mist returning
simultaneously
in two realms
those thirty
incomprehensible days
undeniable
palpable
the Easter clouds
asleep
and awake

Endless Loop

from the satisfied rows of houses
I am separate in my car
listening to Pearl Jam
in the CD player
over and over

stuck in an endless loop
in 1992
when everything seemed to detach
and drift until I decided
under the urgency of emptiness

to drive forever through
the loneliest year
of my life,
which I miss
as if I were not still here

Because

because space is vast
and time infinite
to have spent an hour
in a room with you
in humane discomfort
just the two of us
was a better miracle
than the entropy
and solitude
that awaited us

‡

Ascension

On that late, late night
when you lie awake
and all that was distortion
suddenly is clear

Rejoice, jaded groundwarmer
your mortal wound
is all bled out and
the time to join us draws near

Out in the Cold, Cold Day (2009)

1.
Dear Passerby:
I've been in my cellar so long now
that I have hope again.
I listen to the tone of my voice,
the sound is sincere again.
In a few more days now,
I'll come outside and speak again,
out in the cold, cold day.

2.
Mary had a big old rat who had no fleece at all.
It was matted with congealed blood,
wiry and repulsive to pet.
Though Mary loved her big old rat,
the rat didn't love Mary at all.

3.
Hungry sparrow hopped on the sidewalk
toward a bread crumb lodged in the snow.
Then a crow swooped down and snatched it,
and my brain burned black like coal.

4.
A teacher and her children on a field trip,
out among the dinosaur bones.
Some children shriek;
some are inquisitive;
some drift away from the group,
never to be seen again.

5.
I had a pretty memory of an ex-girlfriend.
On the day we broke up,
I went to the hills and sat in the snow
until I froze.
I had a pretty memory of an ex-girlfriend.
You can still see it on my face.

6.
My neighbor the insomniac
stands outside my door
doing crossword puzzles.
He enters the words down and across,
and plots my death in the margins.
I keep a baseball bat
by my bed, just in case.
I think about buying a taser.

7.
The old world ends each night before bed.
Some look forward to seeing the new world
in the new day ahead.
Some are weary of what
all their days have brought.
"It's always troubled times," they say.
So they lie awake until 4 a.m.,
reading *The Sun Also Rises*.

8.
Reading Abe Lincoln,
shivering in the ruin of the street,
when a pit bull broke loose
from its chain and chased me
until I threw the book at its head.
Now I'm reading Darwin instead.

9.
I went to a diner and sat by a window.
A hobo breathed visible breath onto the glass.
He rubbed his blue arms,
spittle frozen in his beard –
so I looked at the fry cook in the kitchen.

10.
Brokedown Escalade on an icy highway.
I shine a flashlight at the frozen engine
and act the helpful part –
until the darlings inside flash mean grins,
take my car, and depart.

11.
Lost children and pit bulls
roam the world frozen over.
Unable to form an alliance,
they war and starve
and scrape their joints
on the pavement.

12.
When I stare into the mirror for a long time,
my face changes into a lion, then a goat,
and then back to my face again.
Then I feel terror, so I grab
the Book of Revelation off the shelf
and stare frantically at the words.

13.
A monk brews ale in a monastery.
He drinks it with his brothers and says a prayer.
It's a life of sloth, getting drunk without a care,
except for monastery politics.

14.
Abandoned boots out in the ruin of the street,
and a used condom in the gutter nearby;
pieces of a puzzle that,
when I fit them together,
complete the emptiness inside.

15.
Dear Passerby:
Where have the days gone?
Two weeks have passed
and I've done nothing but
sleep with my shoes on.
My resolve is still strong, though,
and my dreams have been godly.
Maybe I'll come outside tomorrow,
out in the cold, cold day.

16.
My neighbor the insomniac
wears lumpy clothes like diapers
over bones with no flesh.
He conceals a vial of anthrax
up his snot-stained sleeve;
a jar of flies in his sagging sweats.
He feeds on doll parts in the morning
and stands outside my door all night long.

17.

I see steel. I see iron.

I see a barge on a river with no music.

I see scaffolding under a gray sky.

I see lifeless eyes.

18.
Couples talking, couples kissing,
couples in mittens walking arm in arm.
It's the second-worst kind of pain
when couples end;
the worst is dying alone.

19.
Crow without conscience
in the tree above my head.
Nothing nice can make
a sound like that.
Unlucky? Not likely.
His kind is all around the world.

20.
Cadillac Escalade with tinted glass,
driving like the plague down my street.
I fill a soda can with pebbles
and bust out the windows,
revealing the darlings inside.

21.
Sitting in a Greyhound bus,
looking at the highway passing by.
Sandbags stacked in fat segments
look like the corpse of a pig.
A strip of tire is a dead snake.
A leather jacket, a motionless coyote.
I take comfort in the sound
of a snoring passenger.

22.
Out in the periphery
is where the lonely hearts go,
inspired by eyes and rain.
They don't ever want to go home,
but they'll vanish if they remain.

23.
A hobo lay face down in the bushes.
His ankles swollen with sores.
The branches were cutting into his flesh,
so I looked at the water in the gutter.

24.
Whenever I see a weak creature get attacked,
the serpent coils around my throat.
Whenever I see a weak creature die,
I curse this world's design.

25.
I hear the sound of sirens
all night long.
Crime of every kind.
Crime all the time.
I have to pay a service
to deliver my groceries.
I have to shave my eyebrows
to shock the postman.

26.
My neighbor the insomniac
put a ladder against my house
and climbed onto my roof,
but he slipped on the icy shingles
and broke his neck on the pavement below.
The sound of it startled me.
The sight of it comforted me.
I slept peacefully through the night
and called the police in the morning.

27.
I gaze out the Greyhound window.
The world is dim like a painting of Poland,
and the day has lost interest in me.
I pass the time looking for meaning
in license plate numbers.
The sun sets on my monotony.

28.
A boy drags an iron chair across cement.
I glare at him until I hear his mongoloid voice
and see his worn-out mother, whose eyes
implore my assistance, which I do not give.

29.
Dead-eyed darlings.
Crows without conscience.
"You stole my car!" I shouted.
Then the crooked cops
showed up and I was arrested
for busting out their windows.

30.
I pled guilty to busting out
the Escalade windows,
said I was sorry to the darlings,
and paid a hefty fine.
Now they drive in my car
with vile grins
and my brain boils black like tar.

31.
Dear Passerby:
I've given this coming outside much thought.
It's been a month already, I know.
But my hope hasn't waned, and will not,
if I stay in my cellar below.
I promise to say a prayer for you
each time you pass by,
out in the cold, cold day.

from Sugar Fish (2007)

Surrender

The bad news kept coming.

He closed shop, receded,

stared at floating dust particles on
Sunday afternoons,

became aware of the give and take
of celestial bodies,
of the thermodynamics of phantoms.

His pupils shined like moonstones.

Friends stopped calling.

At Least There Is a Woman

Here I am
north of Los Angeles
in a café
with an iced coffee
pausing, resting my eyes,
Chopin in the speakers
Rilke's *Book of Images*
spine up on the table.

My stomach is a junkyard;
my lips are dry lamb;
my head a hospital.

I listen to the music.
I contemplate the book.

Yet Los Angeles persists.

At least there is wood and brick.
At least there is cold coffee.
At least there is a woman
standing in the exit looking south,
her left arm resting on her tailbone,
her fingers, heavily ringed,
jingling keys that open the Mazda,
the front and back house doors,
the liquor cabinet,
the desk drawer where the revolver
will remain unused for a lifetime.

White

White,
the salient color of night,
the east and west of human eyes,
the summits of ocean swells and bowling pins,
the bases of waterfalls and baseball diamonds.

White,
the exclusive color of Grecian summers, pensive,
spectral, in rows of sculpture by the hundreds;
the porcelain tinkling of chess pieces,
the sewing of surrender flags.

White,
the crusted color of mummies, insect and human,
the produce of silkworms and of fear,
the effect of quicklime in time of plague,
the priestly smoke of censers.

White,
the obligatory color of doves perched on
clotheslines under black clouds in backyards by
railroad tracks;
the genuine simplicity of respectful observation,
the acceptance, not worship, of irony.

Household Objects, 4th of July

In a plantless apartment of
paper plates and
plastic cups,
street-art oils and
poetry taped to the walls;

in that dark apartment—
windows flung open,
flawed curtains
pulled out by the wind
moving like startled junkies—
a bottle of dish soap
sits on the windowsill.

There for the fifth straight year on
the 4th of July,
it absorbs the sound of fireworks,
as do the isopropyl,
the H_2O_2,
and the reticent spider web
spun and spun again by
generations of hourglass spiders
pleased to repeat the patterns of
their ancestors.

In one corner a
hat rack reveals images of
medicine wheel,
crucifix,

voodoo doll,
skeleton key around its neck.

In another corner a
mannequin looks on,
first mystified,
then elated,
then in hysterics,
mood wholly determined by
flashing pyrotechnics.

Fugitives Count Bullets

Fugitives count bullets on
benches in the forest,

the beetles in the dirt
don't mind.

Giant Times

Daytime moon over downtown Los Angeles:
something big is going to happen tonight.

I plan to hide in the hedge
but instead I wait for dusk
then enter the city with a gun.

Seven blocks to perdition,
I fire at psychotic planes deranging clouds,
bombing towers to the ground;
I fire at demons sucking souls through manholes,
at ghouls ripping tendons off bones.

"Giant times!"
"Giant times!"
I cry to the infernal sky.

And the ashes of my world
flutter by like bats.

Grunge Photos

- For Kurt Cobain

I.
Ticks burrowed into your spine as
you lay on the sofa with your guitar
thinking England 1978.
That was when you were still the boy in
Toughskins who understood punk meant the
Sears catalog and Ecclesiastes.

II.
Mount St. Helens erupted.
The jaundiced sun, obscured by ash,
betrayed you, gave purpose to your infested
bones, that mournful frame of ticks
and iron ore stones
from the banks of the Green River.
You breathed in the volcanic sky,
you smoked some more,
and you swept.

III.
From inside her open casket,
hope sang a power ballad.
You brought her heroin. She offered her arms.
You screwed her on sheets of tar and semen,
the fluids of every generation.
You became perfume and sustenance for famished
magazines, which quoted you saying "One man's

B.O. is another man's lunch."
The magazines said *bless you*.

IV.
Lonely as a reprobate,
uninspired as real estate,
bleak as a Warsaw license plate;
guided by suspicion and charity,
adherent to the principles of bacon,
flannel, and irony,
the gold record on your wall
was the jaundiced sun setting.

V.
All along it was empty space.

About Rain

Hawks' nest in the radar tower,
disintegrating;

he is wandering;

his head receives a crown
of falling thorns.

A black feather;

a touch of gore;

he echoes on the radar screen of lore
like the sound of a thousand cell phones
set to Beethoven.

They call him to the desert plain.

Hawks swoop down,
take back their wooden crown;

black clouds in the autumn sky,
disintegrating;

he is wandering.

Fame

At the foot of a skyscraper of glass,
reflection so searing it could incinerate
entire colonies of ants,
a gull lies on the sidewalk
neck snapped in two.

It thought it was diving,
diving into vertical ocean,
reflection so deep blue, so
salt and cloud,
that it was deceived.

In fact, it was making
the natural transformation
from Narcissus to the Flower,
the precise moment of which
is rarely understood

even among those who can
contemplate the reflection of
their own beauty

before it makes a mess of them
on the sidewalk, in public,
to be gawked at and forgotten,

or sometimes
ignored altogether
by frightened passersby.

Twenty-Seven Observations and a Small Poem About Baseball

If we were immortal, art would be different.

Tuck Everlasting, the Elizabeth Smart story.

Hamburger is truth.

Perfection is a ripe cherry tomato.

Angelyne is JonBenet.

Courtney Love is Ted Hughes.

Impressionism is tempered sadness illuminated.

All study is the study of theology.

The most important bumper sticker says, "My God Loves Your God."

The most important word is mysticism.

The Hitler in us all must be treated with compassion.

MLK, not Malcolm X.

The antidote for psychosis is gratitude.

Like alcoholism, sadomasochism is a progressive
disease.

Doctor, in my current plane of existence, you are
nothing but sound.

Once, a fly at the bottom of my iced tea reminded
me of the 100,000 years of history between ice
ages.

9 x 5 = 45 is the brightest locus in the times table
matrix.

If solitude begins in peace, one may ponder what
might be in heaven;
if solitude begins in turmoil, one may get drunk.

One may regain sanity stirring hot tea with a
wooden stick.

I know to be true that a man once attended the
opera knowing his friend was bleeding to death.

There is nothing more conspicuous than a plain
white van.

My sweaty reflection reminds me of Colonel
Kurtz, the snail, and the razorblade.

All the world adores a self-deprecating midget.

Contempt cannot be bothered with the burden of concentration.

My mind is wicked;
I am not my mind.

Battlements: originally defensive, later decorative.

Compassion is the method;
convergence is the goal.

The final out was recorded
at the night game in Visalia.

The lights turned off.

Moths flew toward the city.

I looked at the stars
and thought:
I'd rather
be here
than
there.

In the Violet Light

In the violet light,
under the towering ferns,
next to the Venus flytraps,
an open pit became a pond of rain water
with lily pads and sugar fish.

Beyond the pond stood a giant sequoia
that was struck by a burning meteor
and burst in shards of color.

There went the dinosaurs...
And I just sat there, grateful and dumbfounded,
a witness to a world that could have happened
two months or a million years ago,
if it happened at all.

Where the sequoia once stood
was a portal that revealed
the nature of the matter,
the nature of loneliness and decrepitude.

What I mean is, it revealed the nature of
my own loneliness
and my own decrepitude.

There went the mammals...
And I just sat there and laughed,
taking refuge in the violet light.

Equal and Opposite Reactions

When anxiety overwhelms,
my mind sees the sterile cafeteria
called Limbo, with
stacked plastic trays, a
silver milk machine, and
carousel horses.

When joy threatens,
my mind sees the hilltop cemetery
called San Francisco, with
narrow cafes,
people looking away, and
eucalyptus in the fog.

When idleness smothers,
my mind sees the lonely helicopter
called July, hovering over
busy playgrounds and
the neighbor's wife singing
skyrockets in flight, afternoon delight.

When morphine drips,
my mind sees the living shrapnel
called sand crabs unable to burrow
into the rug,
their worried eyes imploring me
to flush them down the toilet.

When fear corrodes,
my mind sees the tilted trails
called teetering over the abyss,
a disorienting light in
my helpless eyes
and the humiliating urge to pray.

Who Even Had Time

In retrospect, who even had time to acknowledge the wasted expression on the farmer's face, his transistor radio sitting idle and pointless in the cup holder of his tractor, his tractor doing the same in the barren fields of the twenty-first century.

The Homeless Men

Some arrived from above,
others came from below:
made their debuts as pilots on
sheets of butcher paper
or as dancers fabricated in
cans of cherry soda.

These men passed the time
engaging in the vanity of
solo discourse,
singing massacre in
obscure patches of fog,
giggling terribly,
accusing the crowd of
belonging to this world—
all but the spiders, which
made them wither
like small red leaves in
autumn overcast.

Fish, Hooked

If only
thin atmosphere could pass through gills
without the Being straining for substance.

If only
taut line would snap:

This violent and solitary struggle:
a leap outside the realm,
a passing through to a tribal ritual in the sky.

Like Rotten Tongue

Like a poem by Seamus Heaney,
wormed and hungry;
like a sanguine complexion
well past ripe;
like the gleeful butcher
brooming blood in the gutter;
like so many flies
on heaps of butter.

Like insidious similes
in the hands of surgeons;
like hard-boiled egg
in a beggar's beard;
like a mother's mouth
wishing death to her daughter;
like rotten tongue;
like slaughter.

Goodness

She kept pictures of dead children
(called missing children)
for the sake of holy protest;
kept them like victim trading cards
in a shrine of dry roses and pictures of
living children.

She bore the weight of pill-induced sleep
(called more natural sleep)
for the sake of heavy labor
like the static heft of soil
on nights she tried to die.

She preferred burgundy sheets
taken from the freezer
stretched across sunlit windows;
but she still used perfume
and still flirted with the neighbor's husband
and still cut herself with razors
so goodness could prevail.

Falling at the Farmers Market

Falling at the farmers market:
gelatinous flesh.

Workshirt medics
smack wood on cement.
What a crowd!

They're putting her
on the stretcher.
They're trying.

Healing machines
inches from her leather heart.

Her glasses
on the circular table...

the mesa...

The Colorado River.

Riverbank softens
with the pull of the moon.

External voices.

Fire in the sky.

A cloud.

To the Future Killer Who Might Not Be

What could save you has already happened
and resides in your memory:

curbside Circle K

summer moonlight

the space swept clear
of the day's discarded cigarettes

there you sat

hands on the concrete behind

elbows locked in place

recalling the dream
in which you watered the plants
and woke to the sound of rain.

In the Eye Of

In the eye of the crow
I am a sinister emperor,
a stern yet abundant provider
of carrion.

In the eye of the cat
I am a clumsy insomniac,
affectionate
and easily duped.

In the eye of the hippo
I am disdained like the swan
and deserve to be drowned
on the muddy bottom.

In the eye of the storm
I am a sitting duck
out of luck
with a belly full of minnows.

In the eye of the galaxy
I am a fragile luminary
with skin for burning
bones for breaking
lungs for collapsing
and a deathbed for waking up.

Quietude, a Word

Quietude, a word;
mountain road, an image;
around the bend, a phrase;
a coin.

Elijah, a chair;
mumbo jumbo, a prophecy;
sadness begets clairvoyance, an observation;
a telescope.

Planet earth, an oracle;
land and sea, a strategy;
lion and zebra, a zigzag;
a cigarette.

You, a universe;
of little consequence, a truth;
of no consequence, an untruth;
quietude, a word.

from Poems for Loners
(2010)

1.
When loner was born
he didn't know how to speak,
just like this afternoon
when he woke from a long nap.

2.
Wind and sea
become fog
over the land
and
through the trees
of my dreams.

3.
Loner went down to the water
to exorcise demons from a harlot
and other illusions
only to discover later
that he didn't need to go to such extremes
to get a girlfriend.

4.
The bottle of dish soap I've had
for five years is finally empty.
I'm afraid I've grown attached to it,
but it would be crazy not to throw it away
and get a new bottle.
I know what I'll do.
I'll buy same brand, same size, same color.
No. I'll wander off and never come back.
Hosanna.

5.
Because I'm a human being,
I feel great compassion for others when I see them
all small and nondescript on distant hills.
When others come closer, however, and I can
distinguish voices and personal characteristics, a
lifetime of harsh judgment descends and I retreat.

6.
Monday I watched the day disappear
outside my window
napped on and off with my shoes on
didn't go outside because the museum was closed.

7.
Photographs, postcards, and spider guts
decorate the walls of loner's room.
He watches DVD movies on an old color TV.
He reads many books and magazines but
rarely finishes any of them.
An unabridged dictionary is his preferred surface
for eating and writing.

8.
Some beards are easygoing, with nits.
Other beards hold hateful edicts.

9.
Because I'm a human being,
I linger in gray sky cathedrals.
Original prayer is rare,
but the lines in my face
are more valuable anyway.
Season after season after
season after season
the lines in my face will deepen.

10.
Apostles pass through my fever
sweat on my temples
mouth agape for maximum air.
I lie on a sidewalk lined with eucalyptus.
Crosses, gargoyles, and ice
line the Catholic church across the street.
I want to be Catholic.
I want to believe the Apostles.
I want to love this fever.

11.
One white balloon
in one blue sky
on one green lawn
my body does lie.

12.
In this part of time be gentle.
Then comes pain.
In the next part of time, be gentle still.

13.
Life on earth is dying again.
Come visit me in my childhood home.
In time there will be air again.
In time fish will be reborn in the sea.
But this does not concern me now.
Come visit me in my childhood home.

14.
Peace on earth and goodwill within,
said the bald family man.
Speak freely with the opposite sex.
Have two children.
Watch your two children cross the street
with thirty other children,
hands joined, single file.

15.
Every month or so, loner remembers
two translucent kids from the neighborhood
who died in a plane crash when loner was seven.
When he thinks of them he says,
I will never forget you.
It's the other way around, they say.

16.
Loner went to the aquarium
and secretly cried
when he saw a frowning fish.

Notes from the Graveyard Shift

I.
We sit silently at our stations waiting for work.
There is time to think.
There is time to listen for answers.
We fear what might happen
if we lose our jobs: insomnia, starvation,
the violence on the streets during these hours
which, for us, are hazy and placid.
The halls in our building are dark.
The lights turn off for lack of motion.
There is time to think.
There is time to listen for answers.
We hear the ticking of our watches,
the hum of the air vent.
We think, If death is like the graveyard shift,
that wouldn't be so bad.

II.
Because you are human beings,
you expect vivid descriptions of the character
quirks of we who sit silently at our stations
waiting for work.
We are reluctant to indulge you, however,
because we are skeptical of such descriptions.
We find they are mostly exaggerations and
are sometimes outright lies.
There is nothing phonier than a big personality.
There is nothing more demeaning
than a nickname.

Work with us for a month and you will
appreciate our position on this matter.

III.
There isn't much difference
between night and day.
Both are lit by stars,
as any space traveler knows.

IV.
Preparations for work begin just after sunset.
When the sky has darkened, we prepare our
lunches and then sit as still as possible
to conserve energy.
Listening to classical music is advised.
Reading is not.
You may be surprised to learn that few of us
think of ourselves as night owls and that
most of us are connoisseurs of sunrises,
rather than moon phases.

V.
Lunch hour is at 3 a.m.
We always take lunch in the lunchroom because
we are afraid to leave the building at this hour.
If we take a disagreeable bite,
we are free to spit it into the lunchroom sink
without fear of judgment or reprisal.
We are also free to genuflect and to pray out loud.

When lunch hour is over,
we wash our dishes in silence.

VI.
(4:15 a.m.)
The moths are awake at this hour, orbiting a desk
lamp. They don't believe in night prowlers,
incubi, or succubi. Nor do we.
This shift can make a realist out of anybody.
(4:45 a.m.)
Where did the moths go? Who turned off the
lamp? What was that chill? Those shadows?
Who slammed the door?
Oh, we must have nodded off.
Hosanna.

VII.
On bad nights, we work like satellites,
like drifters in the dark periphery.
On bad nights, we know not to answer voices that
ask, Where is your girlfriend sleeping tonight?
It is better to occupy ourselves with Internet
articles, such as "Hubble Reveals Ghostly Ring of
Dark Matter" or "Mars Experiment Might Help
Earthling Insomniacs."

VIII.
We who sit silently at our stations
waiting for work understand immediately when
one of our own is in trouble.
Just last week one of our security guards
began to obsess on the *Texas Chainsaw Massacre*.
The rest of us called a meeting in the halls,
which caused the lights to turn on,
which gave us an idea for an intervention.
We requested, and our security guard agreed to
three days of intensive light therapy without
sleep. We are happy to report that he now
watches surf movies.

IX.
When the final graveyard shift ended
and we all went under,
we were delighted to discover
more than silent slumber.

X.
We who sat silently at our stations
waiting for work see each other
in daylight in the outside world.
We see each other at beaches
or on park benches in the sun.
We can be spotted all around the world.
A liquid presence surrounds us,

as if we are swimming.
Outsiders catch themselves staring at us.
A curious peace overcomes them.

17.
Loner's hope is revived through freeway culture.
Speed through the future. A river flows.
Alone in the car. A cloud captivates.
Turn the radio dial.
Find a song that suits the cloud.

18.
Don't make fun of Tara.
Her eyes are distant yet intense.
She addresses everyone by first and last name.
She once wore the most beautiful dress
I have ever seen.

19.
There was no dress.
There were thread and fabric.
There was no Tara.
There were memory and mystery.

20.
Trains arrive and trains depart,
either way it breaks my heart.

21.
Too much cleverness
extinguishes the light in the left eye;
too much sarcasm
the light in the right.

22.
Peace on earth and goodwill within,
said the bald family man.
Don't buy bourbon for the crazies
under the freeway.
They'll tear you to pieces
when one of them dies drunk.

23.
Loner brings daisies to the crazies
under the freeway.
Lives are saved
but the mood doesn't change much.

24.
Peace on earth and goodwill within,
said the bald family man.
Bring pennies to the crazies under the freeway.
Listen to them scream.
The sound becomes pure like a choir
and they fly away.

25.
The only way to achieve peace on earth is
to blow up the moon.

26.
The autumn sun was gentle as a folk song
as the soldier passed by my table,
steam rising from my teacup
warm and gray as a
Confederate widow.

27.
Loner is haunted by Latin,
by the pathos of the living past:
Ego tibi memet relinquo, mihi veniam da.
I abandon myself to you, have mercy.
Praeclarus inersque somniare maneo.
Noble and inert, I dream on.

28.
Dark orange flower
in the late afternoon,
what is your name?
I didn't notice you this morning.
I was watching prams pass by
on this path through your garden.
Dark orange flower,
the days are growing longer
for our delight.
Still, no one looks our way.
They smile at the babies instead.

29.
Quit now
hear the girls giggle
the bees buzz for others
O loner
always on the verge of dying.

30.
Whenever loner receives a kiss,
centuries of kisses flash before his eyes.
Awkward loners with melancholy eyes
and fear in their bellies, lashing out for affection.
Whenever loner receives a kiss,
it is difficult for him to maintain his composure.

31.
If asked,
I would say the color of a gull is
white, gray, pewter: a reflection
of the sea.
If asked,
I would say the color of the sea is
blue.

32.
At 5,000 feet,
loner sees tiny creatures battling over
pretty patterns of land.
At 5,000 miles,
loner sees a masterpiece of
color and light.

33.
Like fireflies in the night
I wish you well.

Awards and Acknowledgments

Special thanks to my editors, Jen Richardson, Laura Lionello, and Greg Dalgleish, for their expert guidance in the evolution and completion of this book.

Awards:

"Notes from the Graveyard Shift": First Place, 16th Annual Poetry Super Highway Poetry Contest (2013)

Previous publications:

"Sidetracked," "A Wayward Son," and "You Survived the Ordeal": *Walking Is Still Honest*
"A Laundromat": *Ekphrastia Gone Wild*
"Becoming" and "Because": *Straight Forward Poetry*
"Scorn": *Poetry Breakfast*

"Bakersfield" and "A New City": *The Night Goes On All Night*

"3:36": *The Nervous Breakdown*

"White": *Return from Beyond the Valley of the Contemporary Poets*

"Giant Times": *Misfits' Miscellany*

"In the Violet Light": *Aesthetica* (UK)

"Poems for Loners 3, 4, 5, 20, 23, 31": *Misfits' Miscellany*

"Poems for Loners 6, 11, 12, 16, 17, 30": *Poetry Super Highway*

"Poems for Loners 18, 19, 24, 27": *Media Cake eMagazine*

"Notes from the Graveyard Shift": *Misfits' Miscellany*

About the Author

Douglas Richardson was born on February 20, 1967, in Duluth, Minnesota, and raised in Camarillo, California. He currently lives in Los Angeles, where he works as a proofreader, editor, novelist, and poet.

Also by Weak Creature Press:

Panic Kit by Laura A. Lionello
Panic Kit, Laura A. Lionello's breakout collection of poetry, showcases the author's deft hand and mastery of voice in dealing with universal themes and truths, such as joy, heartache, loss, suffering, and triumph.

ISBN-10: 0984242430 (paper)
ISBN-13: 978-0-9842424-3-6 (paper)

Trust Fund Baby by Douglas Richardson
In *The Corruption of Zachary R.*, book one in his *American Strays* series, Richardson tells the story of Zachary R.'s descent into psychosis and homelessness. In *Trust Fund Baby*, book two in the series, a homeless man is the last thing H. James "Jimmy" Branhoover ever sees.

Who led Jimmy, a young man and the heir to his father's fortune, to such mysterious and tragic circumstances? Richardson goes back in time to Jimmy's early years, examining his relationships with his parents (the well-to-do and good-for-nothing banker H. Charles Branhoover and the former roughhouse prostitute Chloe Red); his childhood cohorts, the otherworldly Kay Sunday and the easygoing Innocent #2; the enigmatic Vander Stevenson; homeless man Charles Larson; and his estranged brother, Bernrd Red.

Tragic, "[a]nd yet, so peculiar, charming, and hilariously funny," the American Strays will challenge and delight readers.

ISBN-10: 0984242457 (paper)
ISBN-13: 978-0-9842424-5-0 (paper)

Ghosts in Time and Space by Douglas Richardson
Richardson's *Ghosts in Time and Space* offers groundwarmers a luminous triptych of memory, emotion, and expression, fortified by unique wisdom borne of experience.

ISBN-10: 0984242449 (paper)
ISBN-13: 978-0-9842424-4-3 (paper)

Poems for Loners by Douglas Richardson
In his fourth enigmatic offering, Douglas Richardson employs poems, lyrics, proverbs, letters, and a diary to illuminate the dark lives of loners.

ISBN-10: 0984242422 (paper)
ISBN-13: 978-0-9842424-2-9 (paper)

The Corruption of Zachary R. by Douglas Richardson
Compunction and collusion drive Zachary R. He harbors disillusionment even while performing life's richest rituals: employment, courtship, marriage, and fatherhood. Memories of a neurotic mother and emotionally austere father shade his adult life with ever-darkening tones. Riddled with madness, he reaches out to those who survive him, those whom he loves, those who will seek to

do him harm. Their collective path to sanity is neither uncomplicated nor without redemption. Who among them will survive the journey?

ISBN-10: 0984242414 (paper)
ISBN-13: 978-0-9842424-1-2 (paper)

Out in the Cold, Cold Day by Douglas Richardson
Poetry chapbook offered exclusively through the publisher. (paper)

All titles offered by Weak Creature Press may be purchased directly from the publisher. Please send an email to **weakcreature@aol.com** for orders or inquiries. Otherwise, you may purchase our titles via online retailers or ask your local bookseller to order them for you.